Heather,

Thank you for being such an amazing person. You definately need your own chapter in the next book.

Enjoy
2022

Page design and typesetting by:
Jennie Dial (jenniedial.com)

Published by:
BK Books Publishing (bkbookshoppe.com)

Follow Kierra on Instagram:
 Instagram.com/rarainks

Follow Krista on Instagram:
 Instagram.com/Krista_Wright_RMT

Issued in print and electronic formats

Softcover ISBN: 9798843464837

Hardcover ISBN: 9798351164618

CONFESSIONS
OF A
MASSAGE TABLE

DEDICATION

I wanted to dedicate this book to my amazing clientele.
Without them, I would not have an amazing career that I love,
and this book would not have been possible.

Thank you.

ACKNOWLEDGMENTS

A special acknowledgment goes out to:

Kierra Boutilier for her phenomenal illustrations. I'm glad I was able to work with her before she becomes famous.

Tarin Glenn for helping me with the first round of proofreading and editing, as well as for emotional support and keeping my sanity occasionally.

A huge Thank You to Jen Dial for the amazing cover page, many rounds of edits, formatting (and reformatting), and basically putting up with me through this whole process.

Barbara Kompik with BKBook Publishing for believing in my dreams and helping to make them a reality.

DISCLAIMER

Massage Therapy in Canada is a branch of the healthcare system. We are listed as paramedical services along with physiotherapy and chiropractic. Most of the provinces in Canada are regulated, and the rest are pushing hard to become regulated entities to protect the clients and the therapists from harm. Therefore, we follow a strict code of conduct which includes confidentiality.

As an active member of two of my province's associations and an active committee member, I have the utmost respect for the privacy act. The people mentioned in my book have provided me with written consent, allowing me to share these stories with you. In addition, their names and any distinguishing characteristics have been removed to further protect their identity. While some of these stories might remind you of someone you know, any similarity to this person is purely coincidental. I can tell you from experience that there is more than one gentleman with a full-back swastika tattoo.

As a final note, this book is meant to be anecdotal and funny. It is about my personal experiences and might not reflect those of other therapists in my profession. Apologies in advance to any massage therapists that may find my humor crass. We all have different levels of comfort, and what I might consider harmless banter another therapist might view as crossing a line or even sexual misconduct. I mean no disrespect to anyone but am just relating my experiences as a massage therapist.

"If there is a book that you want to read, but it hasn't been written yet, then you must write it."

- Toni Morrison , African American author who won a Nobel prize for literature

TABLE OF CONTENTS

Acknowledgments...5

Disclaimer..7

Introduction...13

Chapter 1   Birds... It Had to Be Birds...............................19

Chapter 2   Hot Stone Oops!...23

Chapter 3   Itsy Bitsy Spider...25

Chapter 4   Couple's Massage With Felix...........................27

Chapter 5   Lesson in Compassion.....................................31

Chapter 6   Relationships with Clients..............................35

Chapter 7   The C-Word...37

Chapter 8   Celebrity Massage..43

Chapter 9   Shedding the Sunburned Skins.......................45

Chapter 10   I Smell Something Fishy..................................49

TABLE OF CONTENTS (Cont'd)

Chapter 11   Unintended Affair.................................53

Chapter 12   Snot Rockets.......................................59

Chapter 13   Cat-Cupuncture..................................61

Chapter 14   Identity Theft.....................................65

Chapter 15   Walter...69

Chapter 16   Mini Mouse..73

Chapter 17   Draping mishaps.................................77

CHAPTER 18+ READER
             DISCRETION IS ADVISED.....................81

Chapter 19   Missing Condom.................................89

Chapter 20   G.I. Joe's Toes....................................91

Chapter 21   Underwear..95

Chapter 22   Moan-A-Lisa......................................99

TABLE OF CONTENTS (Cont'd)

Chapter 23   Pumped Up Penis..103

Chapter 24   Let's Talk About Sex Injuries.......................107

Chapter 25   Bite Me...111

Chapter 26   Just the Tip..113

Chapter 27   Suction Problem...117

Chapter 28   Leonard..119

Chapter 29   Wacky Waving Inflatable Tube Man............123

Chapter 30   Happy Ending..129

Chapter 31   The End..131

References...139
.

"The sense of touch is the massage therapist's main avenue used to affect another being and is the body's main method of gathering information about itself. In contrast, an artist uses the sense of vision, and a musician uses the sense of hearing to communicate with others. Touching can affect us physiologically, cognitively, psychologically and emotionally."

~ Susan Salvo, Author of Massage Therapy Principles and Practice

INTRODUCTION

I have wanted to write this book for a very long time. In fact, one of my biggest jokes with clients and co-workers over the years is to say "This is going in the book" whenever something truly cringe-worthy or hilarious happens. I have probably said a thousand times that "someday, I am going to write a book and retire with the royalties."

But, like many others out there, every time I thought about actually writing my thoughts down, my brain would go blank and then the self-doubt would creep in. I mean, do people really want to read about my life? Putting your heart and soul out for others to see (and judge) is a terrifying idea. So, everything I wanted so desperately to share would just sit there in my mind, and I would continue to talk about the book that I would eventually write one of these days...maybe.

Then during one of my massage sessions, the client simply asked, "Why don't you start writing the stories down now, so you'll have them if you ever decide to do the book?" Genius! The idea that I could start writing down the stories without actually planning the book intrigued me. So, after that session, I quickly jotted down what I found amusing during his treatment. A couple of weeks later he booked another appointment, and we chatted about a few more funny moments I had since I last saw him.

After a few months of this, I was given tickets to go see a famous publisher who was doing a seminar on writing and publishing books. Leaving his seminar, I felt brave and empowered as I had never felt before. There were so many stories waiting to be released onto the pages and shared with the world. I couldn't wait to start writing!

I had dreamed about this novel for years. But where do you begin a book? Picking the first story to share was probably the most difficult part of writing this book. The easiest place to start a story was at the beginning... Or what, I believe, was the beginning of my life as a massage therapist.

I have wanted to be a massage therapist for as long as I can remember, even before I ever knew that it was a real job or what it was called. I just somehow knew it was what I needed to do.

In kindergarten (primary) I drew a picture and told my teacher that I wanted to "rub people's backs" for a living, so they would feel better. I had no idea that this was an actual career choice. I just knew that when I wasn't feeling good, or I had a bad day, my mom would rub my back and all my troubles would just melt away. I wanted to share that feeling with the world.

Throughout junior high school, I was frequently in the principal's office for "invading people's personal space" and was often described as "touchy-feely". Not in a creepy way, but I felt most comfortable (and calm) when my hands were touching another person. I loved touching people in a safe and non-sexual way. Of being able to feel the muscles under their skin and manipulating them in such a way that it took away their pain. I loved the idea of being able to connect with someone and being able to heal their body and their soul.

The summer I started high school, my dad was posted to Germany, and I started babysitting for other military families in the area. One of the American wives I was babysitting for did aromatherapy massages in a small studio she had set up in her basement. She offered me a part-time job where I could mind her infant, book clients in, and take payments.

She continuously taught me different industry skills, like the basics of blending aromatherapy oils, as well as additional reception/laundry/cleaning duties that would surround a typical massage therapy business. I loved learning it all and was eager to read through her many books on various modalities, all while the baby napped.

I would "massage" friends and family for fun, trying out the different techniques I had read about and often heard how I should do it professionally. When I came back to Canada for my senior year, I pushed the thought aside thinking massage would be fun, but I needed to think about my future.

While I loved feeling the way muscles worked, I had to focus on something that would pay the bills once I graduated. But then one of the boys I had briefly dated really pushed me to attend an information session at the local Canadian College of Massage and Natural Medicine. He wouldn't let it go. He kept insisting that I should apply, so on the day of their open house I finally agreed to go check them out. I was blown away by the college and the information (and the fact that it was indeed a real job) and I enrolled instantly.

I had to quit my job and move into an apartment in the city with a stranger. Not only that, but I honestly had no idea what I was walking into. There was so much more to massage than just rubbing oil on bodies.

There was learning all about anatomy/physiology/neurology, which we had to memorize down to the cellular level. Even the useless stuff (20 years later I have never touched the inside of an eyeball... But I had to learn it... it's part of the body). We learned pathology, and all about the gross diseases that can happen. So many subjects stuffed down our throats, plus the standard, 2200+ hours of hands-on practice required by our province to graduate.

They were, hands down, the hardest and most stressful years of my life, and honestly, I wouldn't change a thing about it. I have a career I love, an outstanding clientele, and a million stories that I am excited to share. So, find a good spot to curl up, and prepare to be whisked away into the life of a massage therapist. As I share the most hilarious, gut-wrenching, and perverted things that have happened to me over the past two decades, in an industry that is unlike any other.

"Massage is a balance between technical and personal skills, at the heart of which lies the therapeutic relationship. Every time a therapist and a client come together in the context of therapy; this relationship is created. This relationship has a special purpose and goal to serve the needs and best interests of our client."

- Susan Salvo, Author of Mosby's Pathology for Massage Therapists

CHAPTER 1

BIRDS...IT HAD TO BE BIRDS...

In my first "real job" out of massage college, I worked part-time at a small massage and aesthetics business. Emphasis on aesthetics. It had an open concept area filled with a dozen burgundy lounge chairs and carts for manicures and pedicures, a retail and reception corner, and a few treatment rooms towards the back for massage, waxing, and facials.

I didn't really like working there but at the time most spas expected you to have a minimum of two years of experience, which is hard to get if you couldn't find a job. On my first day on the job, I swore I could hear a faint tap-tap-tapping noise that appeared to be coming from either the wall or ceiling, in the corner of my dingy massage room. The noise would come and go randomly, and after a couple of weeks, I started questioning my sanity.

Over time it seemed to be getting louder...but whenever I tried to investigate, trying to locate where it was coming from, it seemed to stop. Finally, after three weeks, I gave up and decided to tune the sound out by focusing on the music, but I kept hearing the tapping...and birds chirping. Birds in spa music aren't all that unusual, but I found it distracting and not at all relaxing. At the end of the massage, I asked the receptionist if she could please switch the music.

Did it work? Of course not! As soon as I took my next client into the room, more birds started chirping! How could anyone relax to the sound of birds? I rushed through her intake and went back to reception again to beg for a different playlist. Preferably without birds! She rolled her eyes at me and proceeded to play music from Enya. Relieved, I thanked her and returned to start the massage on my client. I had just settled into my groove when suddenly the bird noises started again...only this time they seemed more erratic with even more tapping.

My client lifted her head and asked if the chirping was part of the music, just as movement from the corner of the room where the tapping was coming from caught my attention. A small European Starling broke through the ceiling tile, its narrow dark brown body sliding into my room from the hole it had been pecking at. Spreading its triangular wings, it started flying around the cramped dimly lit area struggling to find its bearings. I let out a strangled squeak and flailed as it dove down towards my head. Now off balance, I fell backward off my stool just as it pivoted mid-air and swooped back toward me again, trying to find a way out.

The lady I was massaging (and had completely forgotten about until this moment) jumped off the table, naked except for a little red thong, and started using the top sheet to try and catch it.

We must have caused quite a commotion because soon there

was a knock, followed immediately by the receptionist poking her head through the now slightly opened door. With the additional lighting from the opened door, the small bird aimed itself toward the receptionist. As it dive-bombed her, she screeched and flung the door completely open. The little bird now had full access to the spa. As if this wasn't enough trauma for my day, another Starling peeked out from the hole and decided to join its feathered friend in its terrifying new game of swooping down on their unsuspecting victims as the entire spa erupted into screaming and yelps.

"Massage is the study of anatomy in Braille."

- Jack Meagher, WWII veteran. Author, and Founder of
athletic and equine massage

CHAPTER 2

HOT STONE OOPS!

The day after I completed my Hot Stone training while working at a small clinic, a middle-aged lady booked in with me for a 30-minute hot stone and massage treatment. As this was something new for her, and it was only a half hour, she wanted me to spend the time on her back and opted to keep her jeans and belt on.

When I entered the dimly lit room, she was lying on her stomach, already drifting off. I tucked a warm basalt placement stone under the waist of her jeans to heat her lumbar area as I began rubbing the smooth, heated stones over the tired and achy muscles of her upper back.

I was thankful that she wasn't very chatty because I was so focused on adhering to the routine. I was terrified of dropping a stone or accidentally burning her, and I didn't think I could have held a conversation.

After the massage, I gave her some cool water and home care recommendations. She said my treatment was very relaxing and re-booked for a 90-minute hot stone massage the following month. She left me feeling satisfied with having done a good job and earning a repeat customer.

A couple of hours later, the client called the clinic to say she had one of my stones! It had fallen onto the hardwood floor at her doctor's office...Oops!

"Do your little bit of good where you are. It's those little bits of good put together that overwhelm the world."

- Viola Desmond, Canadian civil and women's rights activist

CHAPTER 3

ITSY BITSY SPIDER

It was roughly 25 minutes into a 90-minute session, and I was just completing work on my client's back when suddenly, a small dark dot caught my eye. At first, I assumed it was just a random floating particle, but as my eyes began to focus on it some more, I realized it was a spider. About the size of my thumbnail, it was casually drifting down from the ceiling directly over my client.

Praying that she wasn't scared of spiders, I briefly closed my eyes before softly clearing my throat and calmly saying, "Umm, I am going to take my hands off you for a second, so I can capture a spider that is about to land on you."

My client whipped her body around faster than I thought humanly possible, while frantically searching for said arachnid until she finally saw it. That's when she let out a blood-curdling shriek and started scooting herself away from it...a motion quickly followed by a yelp as she fell off the table, into a heap on the floor.

I rushed over to her to help her up as she was flailing in the sheets, but the next thing I knew she was screaming and throwing the blankets across the room, leaving me with a fully naked, completely hysterical woman screaming "GET IT OFF!!!! GET IT OFF MEEEE."

The only way I was able to calm her down was to inspect her entire nakedness to ensure sure it was nowhere on her.

"Indulgence comes in all varieties: a mouthful of gourmet chocolate, a hot stone massage, a week in Paris, or 20 uninterrupted minutes to get lost in a book."

- Gina Greenlee, Author, teacher, public speaker, and coach

CHAPTER 4

COUPLE'S MASSAGE WITH FELIX

During the years I worked at a higher-end day spa, there was always something special about the weeks leading up to gift-giving holidays like Christmas or Valentine's Day. Those days were always hectic because, in addition to our regular clients, we always had an influx of people looking to buy gifts or certificates for services for their loved ones, coworkers, etc.

The two days before the holidays, when most people would be finished shopping, was especially busy because that's when a significant number of men would come in looking for last-minute gifts for their partners. During those two days, gift certificate sales would always skyrocket.

Frank, a regular client of mine, was no exception. On this February 13th, he was tapping on the glass door of the spa and frantically waving at me. This was around a half hour after we closed for the night. He had come straight from work to buy a gift certificate for his new girlfriend Sue and had no idea what to get for her. I recommended a romantic couples massage they could enjoy together.

Sue called and booked the couple's massage a few days later for herself and Felix.

Wait? FELIX?? Who is Felix??? Thinking we were dealing with a cheater who had mixed up her Valentine's Day gifts, I was expecting some major drama the day of the appointment.

Because Frank was one of my regular clients (and a pretty decent human who did not deserve to be cheated on), I did not want to be the one to massage her. Thankfully, another massage therapist offered to treat her. I was still needed for Felix as we were fully booked.

Imagine my surprise when Sue shows up at our fancy spa for her couples massage with Felix... a short-haired orange tabby cat. She insisted that she would only stay for the treatment as long as Felix could have a massage too. The owner shrugged it off and told us it was her money, so while my co-worker spent an hour pampering Sue with a lavender vanilla aromatherapy massage and hot towels, I spent my hour being paid to snuggle a kitty.

"Not Actually Felix! Image Source: Shutterstock"

"Soothing touch, whether it be applied to a ruffled cat, a crying infant, or a frightened child, has a universally recognized power to ameliorate the signs of distress. How can it be that we overlook its usefulness on the jangled adult as well? What is it that leads us to assume that the stressed child merely needs 'comforting,' while the stressed adult needs 'medicine'?"

- Deane Juhan, From Job's Body: A Handbook for Bodywork

CHAPTER 5

LESSON IN COMPASSION

S hortly after graduating from massage school, Sara had booked in for a full-body deep tissue massage. The works. After I read her the standard 'undress to comfort level' speech, she responded, "I would prefer to keep my clothes on."

I informed her about the boundary they taught me in school. If there's clothing on, I take it as a 'do not touch zone'. I was not particularly comfortable massaging through clothing and honestly, I was annoyed that she wanted a full-body deep massage but preferred her clothing on.

I'm confident that Sara felt my frustration, and she said, "Oh... ok... I can undress..."

I gave her a few minutes to get settled in. When I tapped on the door and inquired if she was ready, Sara opened the door still completely clothed, with her purse gripped tight in her hands, and a defeated expression, tears streaming down her face. Confused, I asked if she was ok.

She confided she had scars all over, from years of abuse, and just wasn't comfortable revealing them to a stranger. She had never had a massage before, but her psychiatrist recommended trying one to reconnect with her body in a positive situation.

Shocked, I apologized for my abruptness and suggested if she still wanted to try, we could develop a plan to work through her barriers together at her pace.

I felt horrible about the way I made it about myself and my comfort level, and that I thought about Sara's apprehension as being body conscious and not as a trauma response. Since she was choosing to trust me, I needed to give her the special treatment, a heated table, dim lights, tranquil music, etc.

As soon as I introduced compressions on Sara's back, she stiffened up but started to relax as I tenderly kneaded her back through her sweatshirt and the blankets. She decided she was not comfortable having me anywhere near her hips or legs, so I held the sheets as she turned onto her back.

Sara was so nervous her arms were shaking, so I simply brushed over them before proceeding to her neck. When I placed my hands on her shoulders, she started sobbing uncontrollably. Concerned that I was re-traumatizing her, I quietly asked Sara if she needed anything. Between sobs, she said she'd never felt so cared for. This broke my heart. I continued simply to squeeze her shoulders gently until the sobs gradually turned into hiccups before ending the session.

Sara was so grateful that she booked another massage with me a few days later.

I won't lie. I was annoyed at first, but I am thankful that she didn't just rush out in tears, and I learned she wasn't trying to be difficult at all. It was something much, much deeper. With that said, I was knocked down quite a few pegs that day. It reminded me early in my career that everybody has a story. Some are happy, some are sad, and some are full-blown tragedies. I have become more compassionate and open to helping each client heal both physically and emotionally.

"The real purpose of giving massage is to foster more depth of feeling for one another in order to bring out the love that often lies buried beneath the pain of everyday suffering."

- Robert Noah Calvert, Founder and president of Massage Magazine, and author of The International Massage and Bodywork Resource Guide

CHAPTER 6

RELATIONSHIPS WITH CLIENTS

R elationships with clients can be a touchy subject (pun intended).

One of the biggest subjects taught, retaught, and stressed in massage school is maintaining professional boundaries. This means that we always maintain a solely professional relationship with clients. The same rapport that you would have with your doctor or dentist. NO treating friends or family. NO becoming friends with clients. NO socializing outside of the treatment, and DEFINITELY NO dating/sexual relationships with clients.

While I can honestly say that I have never been romantically involved with any of my clientele, I do not agree with the rest of the philosophy. It is human nature to develop an emotional bond when you massage and nurture the same bodies regularly.

Honestly, I feel it is impossible to maintain a solely professional relationship with my regulars. I have a very outgoing personality that typically puts people at ease. I have been treating some of my clients longer than I have even known my husband, and I've been there through their first date jitters, wedding planning, divorces, affairs, pregnancies, miscarriages, cancer diagnoses, death of family members, new jobs... Everything. Some of my clients' children are friends with my kids through school or sports.

I have one client I have been massaging since before she was born. Her mother came to me for prenatal treatments. I was in the room as a doula when she was delivered and gave her very first massage at 30 minutes old. She's now 16, graduating from high school, dating, and I have loved watching her grow up one massage at a time.

And no matter how many times I quoted the textbook that massage is not a substitute for medical care, and I cannot diagnose anything, some individuals would still prefer to ask me before booking an appointment to see their physician. People regard me not only as their massage therapist but also as their friend, their doctor, and their psychologist.

Sometimes the "therapy" is just as important to their healing as the massage. Muscles hold emotions, so why wouldn't you develop an emotional connection to help treat the person as a whole and, as Chuck Wendig so aptly said, not just a magical skeleton filled with meat and animated with electricity and imagination?

"TUESDAY. The day you realize that nothing can stop you, because you are a MAGIC SKELETON packed with MEAT and animated with ELECTRICITY and IMAGINATION. You have a cave in your face full of sharp bones and five tentacles at the end of each arm.

YOU CAN DO <u>ANYTHING</u> MAGIC SKELETON."

- Chuck Wendig

CHAPTER 7

THE C-WORD

I wasn't sure if I wanted to include this chapter, but I promised to show all sides of massage therapy, and this is probably one of those parts of being an emphatic massage therapist that make it the hardest to handle.

Over my career, I have massaged many people, each coming in for something unique to them, whether it's for a deep tissue for a sports injury or lighter touch for acute whiplash. Each person has their own story. A lifetime of overuse injuries and postural imbalances makes everybody different. There are some clients I only see once, then they're gone, while others I will treat 2-3 times a week for years. Those are the ones that stay with me the most, as are the clients that lose their battle with cancer.

It is impossible not to develop a dual relationship (friendship) with my terminal oncology clients and their families. I try my best to keep the boundaries but typically, I will make exceptions and book outside my regular hours, visit them in the hospital for palliative massages, and attend their funeral. And I will cry with them and mourn with their families.

Dual relationships, as defined by the 'CMTO,' is when a massage therapist has some other type of relationship with a client, in addition to the professional therapeutic relationship.

The lines of these multiple relationships sometimes become blurred or merged, making it hard to maintain clear boundaries and distorting or compromising the therapeutic relationship. Examples of dual relationships include, but are not limited to:

1. Personal friendships with clients

2.   Bartering for goods or services with clients

3. Treating family members or

4. Romantic or sexual relationships with clients (which is sexual abuse under the RHPA)

The story I'm about to share is about the most beautiful soul I have ever met. While Joanie cannot give her consent, I have the blessings of her widower and son, whom I have known for many years. I used to work with her son in a coffee shop before I became a massage therapist. We worked the back shift, and we would always stop whatever we were doing to watch the sunrise together.

Our parents turned into fast friends, and his parents would constantly joke about being my future in-laws. Even after I moved away for college, Joanie would often mention, in passing, what her son was doing for work, where he was living, etc. I'm not sure if they were doing the same to him, but in my mind, they were already my second parents.

I barely kept in touch with their son except for the occasional comments on social media. Our parents, however, were best friends. They often vacationed together and eventually retired on the same street. My parents went to his wedding, and his parents came to mine.

About a decade into my career, Joanie had a slip and refused to see anyone else, so I agreed to massage her back and leg. After that, she would book in sporadically when she was in pain. Then one Christmas, Joanie wasn't feeling well. She thought she had a nasty stomach bug and decided to miss the festivities. A few days later, we received the news that it wasn't a stomach bug but an aggressive form of esophagus cancer.

I was devastated. Joanie was not only my second mom and my mom's best friend, but she was also my daughter's partner in crime.

She booked a massage and came in shortly after the Dr. told her she only had a few months left. Joanie needed something that would help her escape the sadness. She needed permission to be sad and angry. We spent that hour laughing at the irony, crying at the injustice, and grieving over the stolen time together.

As her cancer took hold, she could no longer come to the clinic for her appointments, so I would go to her house and massage her in her bed or armchair. Wherever she could find a comfortable position. Some days all she could tolerate was a gentle effleurage to her arms and legs. She would joke about finally reaching her goal weight. It amazed me that she could keep her humor and remain positive even though her body had betrayed her.

When she moved into palliative care at the hospital, I would continue her weekly massages. Each time I walked in was like a slap, seeing such a phenomenal woman melt into this frail frame. We would talk about her life when she was younger, her first spouse, the son she lost at a young age, raising her boys, and meeting her current husband. We talked about all the experiences she had lived through and the events she would miss.

I was with her and her family the day she passed away, gently running my fingertips through her hair. She could no longer talk, but I could sense her body relaxing as each person hugged her goodbye. It was probably one of the most painful moments in my career, and I feel incredibly blessed to have been there with her and that I was able to offer her comfort during her last hours.

"Touch comes before sight, before speech. It is the first language and the last, and it always tells the truth."

- Margaret Atwood, Canadian poet, novelist, literary critic, teacher, environmental activist, and inventor

.

CHAPTER 8

CELEBRITY MASSAGE

During my career as a Massage Therapist, I have massaged a few celebrities.

One actress, in particular, was my favorite because she would jump into unique characters she had played during her treatments. It was like massaging someone with multiple personalities. We made a game of seeing how long it would take me to guess the role. A game I was horrible at, to be honest.

I also love working with musicians. While working at a day spa, I met a few different artists and I even appeared on a TV program on Much Music. That was one of the highlights of my career. An entire camera crew stuffed into my tiny 10×10 room with a Much VJ for a 20-minute staged massage with the vocalist. They interviewed him about how the massage was part of their preparations before a concert at the Metro Center. Then there was a photo opt and CD signing afterward, followed by the actual massage session after the camera crew and fans had left.

Another time, a famous country singer had asked if he could book a two-hour massage starting at 4:30 am. The entire massage was me gently running my fingertips up and down, all over him, similar to a tickle massage but VERY slow. He found this technique would calm his body after a big performance and would schedule an appointment with me whenever he was in town.

"I have a massage when I want to relax. I love being pampered. I love Island massages when you're outside in the fresh air."

- Angela Laverne Brown, Known professionally as Angie Stone. American singer, songwriter, actress, and record producer.

CHAPTER 9

SHEDDING THE SUNBURNED SKIN

L ife as a Massage Therapist is not as glamorous as one would think. I love my career and my clients. Yes, I get some beautiful people to work with, but once they are on the table, my brain switches into professional mode, and I see the muscles and how they work. I no longer look at Mr. Tall, dark and handsome. Instead, I look at the shoulder injury, the misaligned pelvis, and the abuse from overdoing it at the gym.

And then there are those few times when I wish clients had rescheduled their appointments.

Case in point. If you have a sunburn and are peeling, I recommend rescheduling your appointment. Depending on the therapist and the amount of peeling, you may be turned away. Not only is there a risk of infection from the broken skin but peeling someone else's skin off and having it mix with the lotion and roll up into little balls that get stuck to the hands is an unpleasant experience. I do not recommend it to anyone because it's a different sensation.

I have pushed and squished these people pieces around on someone's back. Lots of extended flushing techniques, followed by wiping my palms on the sheets, then casually shaking them onto the floor and trying not to step on them. All while the client was oblivious, enjoying their massage.

Another reason I would ask someone to reschedule an appointment is acne. Now don't get me wrong. Let me be clear on this point. Acne is normal. Countless people experience this, including myself, but when it comes to excessive white and blackheads, these need to be treated by a professional before getting a massage.

For instance, I once had a client who did not mention anything on their intake about back acne. So, as I do with all my clients, I enter the room and dim the lights, do some compressions and rocking before undraping the back, grab some oil and begin warming up their back muscles.

As I began doing some basic Swedish techniques, the oil started feeling clumpy and began to smell rancid. I was concerned I had the wrong bottle, perhaps someone had accidentally mixed oil and lotion? But the smell... it smelled like rotten flesh and disease. As my eyes began to adjust to the dim lighting in the room, I realized the problem was not the lotion. It was the client's back.

Large pus-filled volcanos that were popping and oozing covered their back. And my hands were covered in this toxic goo.

Trying to keep the contents of my stomach on the inside, I excused myself momentarily, letting them know I would require gloves to continue, and scrubbed my hands in the hottest water I could tolerate. Sanitized and double-gloved, I returned to the room where I spent the next 20 minutes maneuvering the minefield and trying not to breathe from my mouth.

"Massage of course is a celebration of the sense of touch and since ancient times this art has found practitioners in almost all cultures, who used it for relaxation, for therapy, for rehabilitation, and for remediation of health problems."

- Dr. Nicholas J Vardaxis

CHAPTER 10

I SMELL SOMETHING "FISHY"

N ova Scotia is a remarkable and beautiful place to live. Every area has a unique view, from the 13,000 km of coastlines to the scenic routes along the Cabot Trail and the vast orchards in the Annapolis Valley. The historical architecture blended with modern buildings makes Halifax a tourist attraction.

Growing up, I traveled a lot, but it seemed like every second posting was back to various bases across this versatile province. So even though I was not born here, I consider Nova Scotia my home. Settling by the coast, I can dip my toes in the Atlantic Ocean on a warm summer day or pick fresh fruit deep in the valley. There is always something to do.

One thing I love most about living here is the little fishing villages. The smell of the saltwater on the breeze mixing with the smell of fish & chips (battered and fried haddock and French fries), vinegar, and the quaint mom-and-pop shops along the boardwalk whisk me away to a simpler time. It's a pleasant break from the bustling city life across the harbor.

The fishermen and women are hard workers and can use the massage, especially during our lobster season. I have treated many people who work in the fishing industry, and typically they are great to deal with, filled with a great sense of humor and stories of the sea, but there was one fisherman who stands out from the rest.

Gil had to be the worst-smelling person I have ever met. When he arrived for his initial massage with me, I almost gagged. Gil smelled like a combination of dead fish, pine sol, and bleach. That first treatment was excruciating, even though Gil was very charismatic. My tiny, windowless massage room quickly filled with his pungent sewer smell. He had come straight from work, and the entire time I massaged his back and legs, I was staring at fish guts smooshed into his pants and a stained t-shirt that hung on a hook next to us.

As I finished working out the muscles on the lower body, I prayed Gil had washed his hands, and thankfully he had. However, he didn't wash them high enough because his forearms had something slimy on them. I had to excuse myself, so I offered Gil a complimentary hot towel aromatherapy add-on. I ran out of the office to grab the towels, added some essential oils, took a deep breath, and returned to the 'bucket of chum' that had become my room. How I survived the hour is a mystery.

No amount of cleaning could get the smell out of the linens. Gil was my last client that Saturday evening, and I was off that Sunday. My office still stunk like spoiled seafood when I came back on Monday. Thankfully, there was some room spray and a diffuser handy.

When Gil scheduled his next massage, I recommended he shower before arriving for the massage to help loosen his muscles. He chuckled and said he was aware of how unpleasant he smelled and his wife "gave him heck for comin' straight from work last time.... But he sure felt outstanding afterward."

A few days later, when Gil arrived for his massage, his hair was still damp from the shower, but the distinct aroma was still there. I could smell his arrival a few moments before I saw him. It was less intense but still noticeable. I knew how badly his muscles needed massaging, and I could not, in good conscience, turn him away because he smelled like a fish market. So, I rubbed some peppermint essential oils under my nose and struggled not to breathe in the smell of sushi as he cheerfully chatted about his day.

I continued to massage Gil, and eventually, his wife started trying different aromatherapy blends on his clothing throughout the fishing season. Orange and cilantro became the winner.

"Even the smallest act of caring for another person is like a drop of water- it will make ripples through the entire pond."

-Jesse and Bryan Matteo

CHAPTER 11

UNINTENDED AFFAIR

There is a point in everyone's lives when rumors take on a life of their own that leaves us floundering in the wake of their aftermath. We become victims of the infamous rumor mill. Whether we are the individual spreading the rumor, or being the topic of interest in said rumor, the need to know (and share) everything bites us all. Humanity seems compelled to spread information concerning each other (usually without fact-checking first).

There's an unexplainable rush of knowing you have the power to share a secret. Sometimes the rumors are small and innocent, like "did you know Susie dyes her hair?" Other times, they can break up marriages, end friendships and destroy trust. Luckily my marriage has open communication as part of our foundation, and I have a good sense of humor. It came in handy when I became a victim of the rumor mill.

For a while, I worked at a larger franchised clinic with nine of the most colorful massage therapists I have ever met. Let's just say there was never a dull moment there. About a year into working at this clinic, a rumor started circulating that I was having an affair with another co-worker by the name of Henry.

Ironically, this rumor started because of a misunderstanding between me, a mutual client named Amber, and a nosy co-worker I shared a wall with. Amber was your average 30-something-year-old woman. Medium build, married, two children, desk job, and gets massages for frequent headaches caused by tension in her neck and shoulders. Typically, she would book her massages every second Friday evening, alternating the appointments between myself and my co-worker, Henry. We would chat a little about how the kids were doing in school, upcoming projects at work, and basic stuff like that during the first few minutes, while I worked to warm up and relax the muscles in her back before settling into what would typically be a soothing massage. She was usually pretty quiet except when I would work out the kinks in her neck.

Then it happened. It was a Friday evening in April, and we were in the middle of our usual early massage chat when she asked me about my plans for the upcoming weekend. I responded that Henry and I were headed to a resort on Oak Island. Before I could even finish my statement...including the fact that we would be picking up two other massage therapists and driving up for an association meeting/conference...she immediately released a huge breath and said, "Oh, thank God! I've been having an affair too!"

She then proceeded to gush about how she had started sleeping with her husband's co-worker after his Christmas party and had had no one she could confide in about it. This secret had been eating away at her for a long time, and now that she had found someone in a similar position who understood, she was all too eager to finally be able to talk.

She spent the rest of her treatment talking excitedly about this other guy, their affair, and how she wanted to leave her husband. As I listened, my head reeled from this new information. At the same time, I also wondered how I would let her know she had misunderstood the situation regarding my co-worker, without making her feel bad.

Awkward? Absolutely! By the end of her treatment, I still had not had the heart to correct her and explain that we were going to the resort as coworkers who were part of a group, not as lovers.

Then, to add to my awkward misery, after the massage, she hugged me and thanked me for letting her get everything off her chest. All I could do was mumble, "no problem," as she bounced her way out toward the receptionist. I immediately went in search of Henry and asked him to meet me in the treatment room for a quick talk while I cleaned it up. I let him know about the accidental white lie, just in case she mentioned it during her next massage with him and continued about my day.

Fast forward to the weekend. We finished up at work and went on to the conference, where I was immersed in new information concerning filing taxes and ways of making a clinical setting feel more like a spa. I had completely forgotten about the earlier events of the day. Unfortunately, unbeknownst to me, Natalie, another massage therapist who had been using the room next to mine during that awkward session, overheard snippets of said discussion regarding Amber and "our affair" and had come to her conclusions. So, while we were busy learning about aromatherapy add-ons and cold stone face massages, Natalie was busy 'massaging' the truth among our coworkers.

The weekend comes to an end and now it's Monday morning. I return to work and go to my treatment room to set up for my day. Natalie comes to find me, props her elbow against the door frame, and asks me how the resort was (and winks).

Puzzled, I told her the meetings went well. "Sure... the conference" (she winks again), she smirks, before strolling out to get her client. Later that day, as I was passing them to greet my client in the waiting area, another massage therapist leaned in and whispered, "Y'know, I've always suspected." Weird. But then not long afterward, another therapist high-fived me as we passed in the hallway. Not sure what to make of those exchanges, I was even more confused when two other coworkers kept glaring at me and would walk out of the staff room every time I went in. I was beginning to wonder if everyone had gone crazy over the weekend. But no. Those random comments, dirty looks, and winks continued all week.

By that Thursday I was beyond confused (and quite irritated by then). That's when the clinic supervisor informed me that we needed to talk and called me into her office where Henry was already sitting with a big goofy smile on his face. My supervisor began the meeting with, "I just want to start this off by saying that I'm very disappointed in you two."

Huh? I started running through all my clients in my head, trying to figure out what I had done wrong. Everyone seemed happy with their treatments. I was receiving excellent reviews and had the highest re-booking rate. Why was she disappointed? And what did it have to do with Henry?

I could feel my anxiety rising in my chest... when suddenly Henry burst into laughter. Now I was even more confused. glanced back and forth between Henry, who was laughing so hard he had tears rolling down his cheeks, and our supervisor, who was standing with her hands on her hips, looking shocked by his response.

It took Henry almost five minutes to calm his laughter and compose himself enough to tell me all about the rumors that had been spreading about us. Rumors that I had been completely oblivious to all week. While they shared a good chuckle about everything, then discussed how best to diffuse these rumors, I just sat there pondering how naïve I had been.

I suppose the saying is true, "I love rumors. I always find out amazing things about myself I never knew!"

"In this hectic life, we have no time to take care of ourselves, hence massage is needed for rejuvenation and stress reduction. A lot of people are looking for quick fixes like, they are taking medications, and they are doing other things which are not healthy. But massage is very holistic and natural."

- Nargis Fakhri, American Actress and Model

CHAPTER 12

SNOT ROCKETS

Most of the time clients book their massages in advance, but occasionally someone will book in on short notice. During my time working at a massage spot in a strip mall, this elegant middle-aged lady booked in for a Swedish massage near the end of my shift.

I will never forget her. She showed up exactly on time, wearing standard business attire, a stylish navy-blue pantsuit, a white starched blouse, bangles on one wrist, and an expensive gold watch on the other. Her hair was in an immaculate bun, not a single strand out of place, and her heels made a stark click, click, click on the tiles as she followed me toward the treatment room.

She was also an impatient lady, tapping her perfectly manicured gel nails on the shelf as I did a quick intake. Typical stress from the office, and tension in the neck and shoulders but would mostly like to relax. Fantastic! I love ending my day with quiet where I can just zone out with the music.

She dozed in and out during the first half of her massage, when she flipped from prone to supine she started sniffling.

This is completely normal as the sinuses don't like being face down. I quietly grabbed the box of tissues and offered her one, but she declined and continued to sniffle. I let her know that the offer was open and to just let me know if she needed one and placed the box on the counter closest to her head (just in case).

Approximately five minutes later as I'm finishing massaging her legs, I looked up just as she blows a giant snot rocket directly into the sheets. She then folded up the sheets a little, laid her head back down, and pretended that nothing happened. I was too stunned to speak. I couldn't believe she actually did that! And then to pretend that she didn't. I thought about how to react and decided not to mention it for the rest of the treatment but was careful to avoid the area.

At the end of the massage, she became irate when there was an unexpected charge to have the linens properly laundered until I explained I had seen her use my sheets instead of the tissues, and asked her if she would be okay with a stranger blowing their nose on her sheets and then leave her to deal with it.

Massage Therapist
[ma'säj 'ther a 'pist] n

A professional miracle worker licensed to create a relaxing ambiance for the reservation of a table for one, dedicated to always having your back, neck, shoulders, arms, glutes, legs, hands, and feet while running on coffee and essential oils.

CHAPTER 13

CAT-CUPUNCTURE

I never expected to have to worry about animals as part of my massage treatments when I first began my career. While there is another branch off the massage tree that concentrates on pets, such as equine (horse) massage, or canine/feline rehabilitation, I remained with human anatomy.

For just over a year, I provided portable massage therapy services. This is where I would bring in my table and all the supplies to your home, hotel, or place of business, etc., so you can enjoy a treatment in a space most convenient for you. Honestly, I could compose an entire novel based on the brief time I offered this. Perhaps I will one day...

One of my very first portable treatments was with a lovely elderly lady named Agnes. She was unable to climb the stairs to the clinic I was working at while she was recovering from hip surgery, so I offered to continue her treatments at her house. She lived in a modest bungalow in a charming suburb, so we arranged for me to come to her place on Saturday afternoon.

When I arrived, I noticed quite a few cats relaxing in her garden and on her veranda, their eyes following me as I walked up the cobblestone pathway to her front door. I shrugged it off, figuring she's old and lives alone, so she probably feeds the strays. I knocked on the door and as soon as she opened it; I was slapped in the face with the pungent smell of filthy cat litter and old nicotine.

Agnes ushered me in hastily, while some cats dashed out and others came in at a leisurely pace. Talking to the cats, she pointed towards an area in the outdated living room where I could set up while she hobbled into the kitchen to "feed her babies". I counted at least another eight cats, perhaps more, while setting up my portable massage table among the braver ones and the flowery furniture that has been thoroughly and utterly destroyed by the cats' scratches.

During the treatment, there were cats twirling around my ankles, climbing onto the table, wandering up and down her back, and brushing against my arms while I was trying to massage her. One was even trying to lick the coconut oil off her back as I was applying it. When I re-draped her back and started massaging her hip, yet another cat jumped up and started kneading intently between her shoulders. Agnes simply chuckled and commented how it was like having an acupuncture treatment and a massage at the same time. We called it her cat-cupuncture massage.

She had a total of 27 cats!

"Massage is the only form of physical pleasure to which nature forgot to attach consequences."

- Robert Breault, American Operatic Tenor

CHAPTER 14

IDENTITY THEFT

A woman about my age and build scheduled in with me for a full-body massage. During the intake, she informed me she used to be a masseuse before having to quit because of a sore wrist. I thought this was unusual, as most massage therapists adamantly shun the title masseuse. It is often associated with prostitution, happy endings, untrained therapists, etc. But I brushed it off. Maybe she studied outside of Canada? Either way, it's not a serious deal to me personally.

During the treatment, she declared "her wings always hurt at the end of the day"... It took a couple of minutes to work out that her "wings" were her scapula bones (also generally referred to as shoulder blades). Another red flag popped up in my head. Anatomy is an extensive part of our education.

I chatted with her about other areas that were bothering her and the possible onset of the injuries. I couldn't shake the feeling that she was hiding something, so I began inquiring about her massage career. She was strangely vague about where she had worked, and how long ago she left the industry. She simply repeated that she used to be a massage therapist but left due to an injured wrist (but then asked me to skip her arms). Whatever, it's her hour.

Instead, she was curious to know how long I have been practicing, where I took my training, and just really interested in "talking to someone who's still in the biz"... I finished the massage and was thrilled that she didn't rebook.

A week later, a friend called me because she saw my name on the schedule at the spa where she works. This "client" copied my bio and used the information we talked about to BS her way through the interview. What a headache it was. I had to cancel my clients for the day and go into the spa to prove that I am myself and she was trying to steal my identity to get a job.

I am just thankful that somebody told me before she did some major damage to my reputation and to clients.

"The difference between a rubdown and a massage is an art form called accuracy."

- Jack Meagher, Medic in General Patton's Third Army during WWII

CHAPTER 15

WALTER

Walter was an older man whom I had seen a handful of times for general massages, mostly to help with the typical aches and pains that come with age. He had come in for a relaxing massage two days after having a colonoscopy. Before we started treatment, he informed me he had been having 'some residual gas' since, and he left his underwear on.

I told him that the flatulence after the scope is completely normal and doesn't bother me. To make both of us feel better, I used some office spray and made the small room smell like "Tahiti Sunset" before beginning the massage. As I was working out a knot in his lower back, he let go a couple of farts and blamed it on low-flying ducks overhead.

As he was turning over, he let out a HUGE gaseous cloud and got this weird look on his face.

Walter: "Um, excuse me, dear. Could you please leave the room for a couple of minutes?

Me: "Sure, are you ok Walter?"

Walter: "Well, ma'am, no. Quite honestly, I am not ok.... I need to cut this thing short... That was NOT gas." Me: "Oh? ... OH! ... Um... Ok, stay right there. I will be back with some wipes."

Walter was beyond mortified! He took an entire package of baby wipes, a garbage bag, and the sheets. Then he left $100 on the table.

It took him almost two years before he came in for another massage with me. Determined not to let it be awkward between us, I made a joke saying, "I promise this massage won't be as shitty as the last one." Walter looked at me and burst out laughing.

When I told "Walter" I was writing this book, he told me he deserves a chapter and chose the name "Walter" as his alter-ego because of the doll Jeff Dunham uses.

THE MYSTERIES OF ANATOMY

A brilliantly written verse for lovers of the English language

"Where can a man buy a cap for his knee,
Or the key to a lock of his hair?
Can his eyes be called an academy?
Because there are pupils there?

In the crown of your head can jewels be found?
Who crosses the bridge of your nose?
If you wanted to shingle the roof of your mouth,
Would you use the nails on your toes?

Can you sit in the shade of the palm of your hand,
Or beat on the drum of your ear?
Can the calf in your leg get the corn off your toe?
Then why not grow corn on the ear?

Can the crook in your elbow be sent to jail?
If so, what did he do?
How do you sharpen your shoulder blades?
I'll be darned if I know. Do you?"

- Author Unknown

"I take a massage each week. This isn't an indulgence, it's an investment in your full creative expression/productivity/passion and sustained good health."

- Robin S. Sharma. Canadian Self-help Writer

CHAPTER 16

MINI MOUSE

The year was 2006 (I think). I was working in a small clinic located in a small plaza. It was your standard strip mall then, with a bookstore, a pet store, a dozen other mini-shops, and a limited food court. The clinic I worked at was upstairs, next to an optometrist's office and a cramped seating area that was mostly occupied by pensioners who liked to people-watch and gossip while sipping their coffee.

As I was giving a two-hour massage one afternoon, I heard a rustling noise coming from the direction of my client's things. At first, I dismissed the noise as simply being the seniors shifting in their chairs in the sitting area on the other side of the wall. Between the client chatting and the music, it was a little hard to tell.

A short while later, my client was drifting off to sleep, while I was rubbing her feet and I noticed a movement by her purse. While I was trying to figure out what was moving, a small tan-colored mouse climbed out of her bag and onto the ottoman, then just sat there like it belonged in my room. As I'm deciding if I should run away, or how I could transition around the massage table to reach it without disrupting the treatment, the rodent jumps off the ottoman and scurries under the table.

So, here I was, struggling to continue the massage while searching for a flipping mouse! I somehow managed to catch it under a hand cloth, toss it into my (thankfully) empty garbage can, and put a textbook on top of it, all while keeping one palm on my sleeping client and trying not to scream. I grabbed some hand sanitizer off the shelf, then turned my client over and continued with her massage as if nothing had happened.

Eventually, I forgot about it... Two hours is a long time during a quiet massage. Five minutes after I finished the session, and she had checked out, she came rushing back into my clinic freaking out because her son's pet mouse had been in a paper bag in her purse, and it was gone. We both ran into my room, and he was still at the bottom of the garbage can where he had fallen asleep.

The mouse was fine, and she was thankful that I had found him, but I had to ask, "Who the hell keeps a pet mouse in their purse?"

*"They say you can't buy happiness, BUT you can buy
a massage, and that's the same kind of thing."*

-Unknown

CHAPTER 17

DRAPING MISHAPS

The word "draping" in massage refers to how a massage therapist covers an individual with sheets to allow the therapist access to the various parts of the body while still protecting the client's modesty.

There are many philosophies about massage draping around the world. Some drape conservatively and provide full-body coverage, while others might give you a facecloth (if you're lucky). In Canada, we take the more conservative approach. A professional establishment will have a face cradle covering, a bottom sheet, a top sheet, and typically a blanket.

A massage therapist must have permission (and reason) to expose any section of the client's body apart from the head. The art of draping is an essential skill for massage therapists taught throughout our training. And while uncovering a person's limb seems pretty basic, it's not as easy as it appears. Quick and efficient draping is a vital part of a relaxing massage. The sheet had to be secure, with boundaries that separate areas treated from those that were not while preventing exposure to the client. You don't want your therapist to accidentally uncover your "goods" or spend 20 minutes "tucking you in."

The therapist must adjust draping through assessment or treatment to ensure that only the areas of the body that are receiving a massage remain uncovered. In some places, sensitive areas (Breast, bum, and stomach) require written consent to be undraped or treated. We are never to expose the client's genital area or gluteal cleft (aka butt crack).

Every so often, I would treat clients who didn't want the sheets. I sometimes removed the blanket, but the top sheet was non-negotiable. For the clients that commented, "You have kids, so you have seen one before," or "we're both women, it's not like I have different parts than you," I simply responded with, "If you have something I haven't 'seen' then please show me now and then go straight to the emergency hospital to have it removed," which usually gets me a laugh. I can then explain why we require sheets in our province. Also, besides it being the law, even if you have no modesty, that doesn't mean I have to be subject to your anatomy. Some things need to be left to the imagination.

I don't believe every client uncomfortable with the full draping is a potential pervert. Most of the time (for me anyway), the clients stripping off the sheets were middle-aged women experiencing power surges. But on some occasions, draping mishaps do happen. I have been 'flashed' by so many women trying to cool themselves that I am convinced this is how hot flashes got their name. I have also had moments when the client is rolling over, where they become twisted in the sheets like a burrito or dump them all onto the floor.

And while I do have a blurb for new clients that goes something like, "AFTER I leave the office, undress to your comfort level, lay on your stomach on top of the bottom sheet, covering yourself with the top sheets. Do you have questions before I step out?" Occasionally, clients don't understand (or care). They will start stripping off while I am still talking. Or tell me I can come back in, and when I open the door, they are still in the process of undressing. Or be found wandering around the room naked.

Also, on occasion, I will return to find them laying on top of everything, hairy arse up. Once I walked into my treatment room to find my client, a woman, lying knees-up and spread wide open like she was preparing for a pap test. Before spinning around and directing her to please get under the sheets, I got an up close, and personal view of her 'money shot' in all its glory.

But the one that takes the prize is the lady who decided to remove all the sheets, toga herself with one of them, refold the rest, then lay on top of the bare table.

"Benefits of massage: Promotes deeper breathing, improves posture, improves circulation, enhances skin tone and skin health, increases and promotes joint flexibility, enhances a calm mind, reduces anxiety, increases self-awareness, promotes mental alertness, increases peace of mind."

- Unknown

CHAPTER 18+

READER DISCRETION IS ADVISED

Before getting into the stories that you have been waiting to read...the main reason why 90% of you probably bought this book, I would like to take a minute to discuss why chapter 18+ is "Reader discretion is advised."

Like all massage therapists, I put up with a seemingly endless stream of "happy ending" jokes. I hear them from clients, friends, and family members, both at work and while out. It's typically the first thing someone asks upon hearing what I do for a living. "You're a masseuse? Do guys ever ask for happy endings???" The simple answer is yes. Yes, they do.

Personally, I am not bothered by these questions, comments, or innuendos. But some therapists have a zero-tolerance policy and do not feel these jokes are hilarious, or even acceptable. And, unfortunately, the reality is that every massage therapist I have met has had to deal with a few sexually... heightened moments with clients over the course of his/her/ their career. In fact, a study done this year (2022) in Canada has shown that over 80% of massage therapists have been sexually harassed during their careers.

Most of the time, the harassment is verbal, and a simple conversation can correct the behavior, but sometimes it goes beyond joking and the therapists have been left shaken and in tears, questioning themselves. A few great people I knew have even left the career they loved as a result of some egomaniac who thinks everyone wants to touch his dick.

I am not saying men should be ashamed of getting erections. Or that the massage will end the second your sailor stands at attention. Getting a hard-on during a massage appointment is normal. It happens. So, to all the guys out there: You don't need to be embarrassed. There is no need to end your treatment immediately and dart out of the room like a teenager after his first chubby in class.

Most massage therapists are professionals and won't just stare at your tent. We really don't want you to feel any more uncomfortable than you already are. So just relax -- and know that as long as you don't make it dance or wave like an inflatable tube man under the sheets, we are not judging (or secretly condemning) you.

That said, there are some lines that shouldn't be crossed.

1.   There Is No Need for Show and Tell

"Wow sir, I see you have an enormous erection!"

How might I know this? Because you have ever-so-unkindly removed the blanket that was (purposefully) placed on top of you to make absolutely certain that I am aware of your arousal. And then to add to my misery you want to draw more attention by talking about it, repeatedly touching yourself, or my favorite...by making it wiggle around!?

Do you know what I'm thinking during this game of show and tell? No. I **do not** want to play peek-a-boo. I am thinking that I want to end the massage immediately. Although, if you make this mistake, I typically offer you the chance to take the hint that this behavior is not OK by placing another blanket (or large poofy pillow) on top of you, all while silently praying that this is where your shameless peacocking display ends. If not, though -- be prepared for me to call you out on it in the same mannerisms of a catholic nun.

2.   **Please Do Not Give Directions to Your Penis**

If a guy is sporting some wood and asks me to massage his inner thighs or lower stomach, guess what? Despite being born a blonde, I am not stupid. You might be surprised to know massage therapists study anatomy extensively and do know what you are not-so-subtly hinting at. You are fooling no one, Sir.

Do you honestly think my hand is going to magically start tugging on it because you are inviting me to massage around where Peter Penis hangs out? Uh, nope. Hard Pass. Trust me, I do not get paid enough and you are definitely not worth risking my career, or my marriage, over. You will likely receive a less-than-average-level massage, with a lot of elbows digging into those sensitive areas.

3.   **Please, Please Do Not Hump My Table**

No, really, this actually happens to me at least a couple of times per year. Typically, from male clients, but I have had women grind their hips around the table as well. If a client is aroused, and then his/her position is switched to lying on their stomach, they might start humping the table. Dry Humping or "purposeful wiggling" -- however you want to term it -- is a sexual act that is just awkward for both of us.

I understand a client's need to adjust, especially men since their genitals are external, and I have been told laying on a raging boner is uncomfortable, to say the least. But you should only need to "adjust" yourself once or maybe even twice. Anything more than that is inappropriate. And please show some respect! do not hump the table until you are "satisfied" leaving a cold sticky puddle for me to clean.

4.   **Do Not Touch the Therapist**

If you absolutely must become aroused during your massage and start thinking dirty thoughts, then please apply the same rules as in a fancy strip club. Enjoy... but No Touching!!!!! Especially while you have rigor mortis in your purple-headed yogurt slinger.

Honestly, unless you are having a stroke or heart attack, or you're choking on your gum, please do not touch your massage therapist. My job is literally touching you in a non-sexual, therapeutic manner. Your job is to lay there and take it. Just relax. Don't try to figure out how you can rub my legs or touch my ass "accidentally of course". And definitely do not try to sniff my crotch like a dog as I move around the table.

Again, exceptions to the rule: Depending on the therapist, some touching is appropriate: shaking hands before/after your treatment. And perhaps, if you are an established regular with your therapist, hugs might be acceptable. A lot of my clients like to hug, and I am ok with it, but again, another therapist might not be.

And my own personal request...

5.   **Please Masturbate Before (Not During) Your Appointment**

Yes, you read that correctly. Just so no one is confused: This is something I am personally asking you to do. Listen, the reality is, that sometimes clients do ejaculate during appointments. Sometimes it is obvious during the massage, and sometimes they leave their "gift" for me to find... and these incidents are where newer (or seasoned) therapists will spend eternity retracing what they did during the massage, and was there anything that could have prevented it? So, if you are one of those people (either purposely or by accident) then I am asking you to rub one out and empty the chamber before getting on my table.

The standard protocol for this type of behavior is for the client to be banned from returning to the spa/clinic ever again. And this probably goes without saying: if the therapist has to terminate your treatment early Everyone at the front desk will look at you like a creep as you weasel your way out the front door. Depending on the severity, the police might also become involved.

Now how is that for your happy ending?

To my fellow massage therapists: Please, please remember that if this happens during one of your services, it was not your fault. And on that note, please enjoy all the perverted and disgusting moments that have made me the twisted person I am today.

A really good friend of mine posted this to my Facebook trying to be inspirational and help to motivate me to complete this book. Meanwhile, for me... The context is completely different, so I had to include it.

"You can't just hope for Happy Endings. You have to believe in them. Then do the work, take the risks."

- Nora Roberts, American Romance Author

CHAPTER 19

MISSING CONDOM

My first job out of college, I had a male client tell me during the intake that sometimes he ejaculates accidentally during massages, and it has caused problems in the past. His wife recommended that he wear a condom during the treatment. This way, I wouldn't have to clean the wet spot.

I explained that I only offer therapeutic massage and after speaking with him more I had no other indications that he would be looking for "other services," so I agreed to proceed with the treatment. I treated him a few times, and he was a fantastic client, but after one massage he informs me that he lost the condom!!!

I was freaking out for hours because I had shared a treatment room with my boss and was terrified that I was going to be fired or arrested for prostitution.

Near the end of my shift, the receptionist found it... in the lobby... stuck to the bottom of my shoe...

"A man too busy to take care of his health is like a mechanic too busy to take care of his tools."

– Spanish Proverb

CHAPTER 20

G.I. JOE'S TOES

There are few places in the world where someone feels thoroughly at ease and comfortable discussing anything without fretting about what the other individual might think or say. I believe that the massage room is one of those places. Massage is like a personal psychiatrist mixed with a bartender. It's a wonderful place to unwind, physically, emotionally, spiritually, and mentally. But sadly, we don't provide alcohol.

"It's actually Massage AND Therapy" ...I will often joke when a client over shares something personal that they wouldn't usually talk about, specifically with a stranger.

This is the story of Joe, and his army boot toes.

The first time I met Joe, he shared one of these exceedingly personal stories with me. He had gone for a massage three years prior and had never been back.

While he was overseas for work, a couple of army buddies were going to get massages to unwind while they were on furlough and persuaded him to join. So, he went with them thinking he would book in for a nice, gentle, relaxation massage like his wife goes to the spa for. The tiny Asian massage therapist did not understand much English. She immediately went to pull down his boxers and he quickly informed her he just wanted a regular massage. After an

awkward couple of minutes of trying to explain what he
wanted she started kneading the muscles on his legs.

Her approach was extremely rough and quite painful. She
found knots in the muscles of his back and dug them out with
her fists and elbows like she was trying to tear the meat from
his bones and exorcise his inner demons.

After the hour finally ended, Joe met his comrades outside
and told them about the awful experience. The other guys
laughed, and they told him this was a place to schedule a
different type of massage that didn't actually include very
much "massaging" ...If you know what they meant. He had
made a sex worker perform a massage and she was less than
happy about it.

For weeks, Joe was covered with large purplish bruises on his
body that hurt whenever he moved and affected his job
performance. He developed some major trust issues with
letting anyone touch him. These issues seeped into other areas
of his life, and despite going to therapy, Joe, and his wife soon
separated.

The following year, he met Amy, a regular client of mine at
the time. She was a fiery redhead, who was into BDSM. She
was completely different and introduced him to the
pain/pleasure concept, communication, and consent. She
compared massage to foreplay. At 14, Joe's first experience
kissing a girl was sloppy and awkward, and he didn't
understand what the appeal was. But as he matured, he dated
other women, and kissing became something more. Similarly,
the Asian woman had rushed in without any "foreplay" and
he did not enjoy it, but that doesn't mean he should never try
again. Amy had opened his eyes (and his pants) to a whole
new world of possibilities. One of the things he determined is

that he really enjoys having his toes sucked on after marching in army boots all day.

Somehow, Amy and this new kink had given Joe the courage to step out of his comfort zone and give massage another try.

I learned all of this within the first appointment with him, simply by asking if he has ever had a massage before... it was a lot to take in.

Ultimately, I am glad that Amy convinced him to allow massage therapy another chance, with the understanding that it's all about communication and finding a therapist who suits your personal needs. And I am especially thankful that I was the therapist he booked in with. I feel like he needed to get this story out in order to move on. Every therapist is different, and another person might not have listened. In our profession, we started with the same tools in our toolbox, but as we practice and learn new techniques, our styles change. I was able to work with his trauma and develop a treatment style that works for him.

Joe has become a fantastic and loyal client who has only ever asked me to suck on his toes once... and has graciously agreed never to ask again.

*"Massage has a positive effect on any medical
condition we've looked at."*

- Tiffany Field, Ph.D, Director, Touch Research Institute,
University of Miami

CHAPTER 21

UNDERWEAR

This is a conversation that I've had with a new client on more than one occasion:

Me: "I'm going to step out to wash my hands. Please undress to your comfort level, lay on your stomach under the sheets, with your head in the face cradle."

Client: "Should I wear underwear during my massage?"

Me: "Whichever you are most comfortable with."

Client: "Which do you prefer?"

Me: "Personally, I prefer none. It helps me access the glute region more easily."

Client: "Glute?"

Me: "The bum."

Client: "Ok, I wasn't sure, so I brought a pair with me just in case."

Every once in a while, I have moments where I'm like, "Wow... This is my life! It is appropriate for me to tell someone not to wear their underwear so it's easier for me to touch their butt."

"I love a massage. I'd go every day if I could. I don't need to be wrapped in herbs like a salmon fillet, but I do love a massage."

- Jason Bateman, American actor, Director and Producer

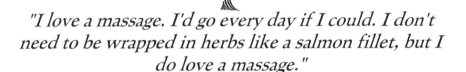

CHAPTER 22

MOAN-A-LISA

Lisa was a very quiet, petite, 20-something-year-old college student whom I would treat once a week for 75 minutes and preferred a deeper massage. I remember the first massage with her like it was yesterday. She had called and requested our latest appointment and was very apprehensive on the phone about crossing paths with other clients. I found her a spot where she would be the only client in the clinic because she was so anxious.

She arrived ten minutes early and sat patiently with her hands folded in her lap, staring at the wall, trying extremely hard not to form eye contact with my receptionist. Dressed in business-casual attire, she informed me she had come straight from work. Lisa had the softest voice. I felt sad, wondering what would cause such a gentle and sweet young girl to be so timid about coming in for a massage when others could see her. During the intake, the air conditioner was running, and I had a rough time hearing her because she spoke barely above a whisper.

Although she was a quiet conversationalist, she sure discovered her voice during her massage!!!!! As I worked on Lisa's lower back, she let out the longest deep-throated moan I had ever heard. Was I hurting her? I checked in. No. She was fine. A minute later, she lets out another long moan, and another. These moans sounded like a cross between pleasure and pain and they were LOUD, with the occasional whimper and gasps as I found knots.

As I proceeded with the treatment, Lisa's moans turned into what I can only describe as sex cries. I was incredibly thankful I had accommodated her and created a spot where there were no other treatments happening. Since we were alone, and she was my last client of the night, I continued the massage while she whimpered and pleaded and screamed in ecstasy. When the massage finally ended, I slipped out of the room and the receptionist wiggled his eyebrows at me and quietly applauded.

Lisa emerged from the office a moment later, back in her quiet persona, smoothed the front of her skirt, and thanked me for a fantastic treatment and for not making her feel uncomfortable with her "vocal outbursts."

This became the norm during her massage, and I expected this expressive release every week when I would massage her. Three years into treatment, shortly after her college graduation, she tells me she was working as a phone sex operator and did some amateur porn to help pay for college. She would book her massages on nights she worked because her voice was raspier after a good rub down.

"Touch was never meant to be a luxury. It is a basic human need. It is an action that validates life and gives hope to both the receiver and the giver. The healing of touch is reciprocal."

- Irene Smith, Classical Composer and Educator

CHAPTER 23

PUMPED UP PENIS

I had an older gentleman in his mid-70s check in for a massage. About twenty minutes into his massage, he randomly informs me of the penile implant surgery he'd had a couple of months prior. He then went on to explain to me that he has the inflatable model... which, as he happily described, was a fluid-filled sack implanted under his abdominal wall with a pump and release valves placed inside his scrotum and two inflatable barrels inside his penis.

It meant that whenever he wanted an erection, he could simply pump or squeeze his ball sack repeatedly, which would cause the saltwater in the reservoir to flow into the cylinders inside his member.... I mumbled that I had learned something new today, and continued his massage, praying under my breath that he would drop the subject.

A couple of awkward minutes later, he asks me if I would like him to show me how it works...

I answered very professionally, stating, "While the medical advances for erectile dysfunction are interesting... no, I do not need to see how it works."

Then he said, "I can show you from an educational standpoint. It doesn't have to be weird!"

To which I responded in a much firmer and my best mom's voice, "I do not want to see how you can pump up your penis! Please stop asking!!!!!."

The rest of the massage was blissfully quiet.

"Massage is the only form of physical pleasure to which nature forgot to attach consequences."

- Robert Breault, American Operatic Tenor

CHAPTER 24

LET'S TALK ABOUT SEX INJURIES

I have seen quite a few sex-related injuries in my career. Some clients are embarrassed, and some are proud. But occasionally, one catches me by surprise.

I had a lady come in for her massage appointment with a very swollen, purple jaw. She was complaining of soreness in her neck and upper back. And, of course, she was hoping I could also help with her jaw. After asking her a few questions regarding the injury, I could see she was nervous. She was being evasive, so I decided not to push the issue. Since she could not put any pressure on her face, we agreed to do the entire 45-minute session in supine, and as I worked out the muscles in her neck and upper back, she relaxed.

I started doing superficial massage strokes around her jawline to help reduce the swelling, but as soon as I felt the muscles, I had to ask questions. What had happened? How long had it been inflamed?

The temporomandibular joint (the hinge where the lower jawbone connects to the skull) felt misaligned, and I had to be super gentle because of the injuries. It took some time, but I lessened the pain along with the swelling and regained some of her movement.

She was vague about her answers, and the more I massaged around the area, the more I suspected spousal abuse. As calmly as I could muster, I advised her she didn't have to disclose anything to me if she was uncomfortable. I recommended speaking to someone when suddenly she blurted out, "My husband was taking me from behind, and when I looked back at him, my face smashed into the edge of our headboard."

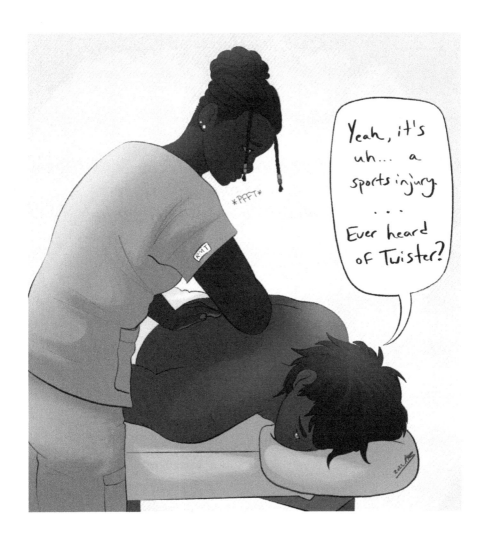

"The fact that my entire body cracks like a glow stick whenever I move and yet refuses to actually glow is very disappointing!"

- Unknown

CHAPTER 25

BITE ME

A couple of years ago, there was an internet sensation called Dr. Dot.

She was a massage therapist in America who would bite her clients (mostly celebrities) as a way to work into the muscles.

I had one particular gentleman ask if I was familiar with her.

I told him I have seen her videos. A couple of moments later, he inquired if I would consider biting his back and thighs. First off, he was exceptionally hairy. Secondly, that is way outside my scope of practice. Lastly, there is not enough Listerine in the world.

He seemed to accept this answer until his next massage when he asked if I would shave his back. Or perhaps he could get it professionally waxed and would come in freshly showered. He really wanted to try the biting massage. Again, my answer was, "Not gonna happen!"

The last time I saw him, he offered me $50 for every bite mark I left on his skin. Occasionally I wonder how much I could have made.

"Sometimes the best thing to do is to call it a day and go get a massage."

- Unknown

CHAPTER 26

SUCTION PROBLEMS

I n this new episode of a couple's massage with a new therapist...

I was scheduled to work with the woman, while my co-worker had her boyfriend. As was standard routine, we greeted the couple at the reception area, introduced ourselves, and asked if either would like to use the restroom before leading them to the duet room. As we walked down the narrow hallway, my client appeared to almost cling to her man. It made me think that she might not be comfortable with another woman working on him. But since she wasn't saying anything, neither did we. We completed our intake and stepped out to wash our hands while the couple undressed.

Now at that particular spa, we were required to do everything in sync. We would begin the treatment with the clients laying on their stomachs with their faces resting in the face cradle, then about halfway through the process, we would instruct them to turn onto their backs at the same time to complete the rest of the treatment. These were meant for relaxation with minimal distractions.

I was really looking forward to turning my brain off for an hour as these were always relatively easy treatments, until the other therapist joined me, lugging a one gallon (3.79 liters) jug of oil, instead of dispensing it into a smaller bottle. And just to make matters worse, the pump on her jug didn't fit quite right, and it made this weird, wet, sucking noise every time she pumped oil from it. Every time my co-worker pumped that bottle, my client, who was lying face down, would twitch. She would not relax because she was convinced something shady was happening between the other therapist and her boyfriend, WHILE SHE WAS IN THE ROOM!

So, at halftime, I signaled to my co-worker that it was time to turn them onto their backs. As they were in the process of flipping over, my lady got up, fully naked, and attempted to slide in next to her beau on the narrow massage table while he was still in mid-flip! His whole body stiffened! You could tell he had no clue what was happening.

I was trying so hard not to laugh (and failing miserably), and my co-worker looked over at me mortified. I gave it a minute to see where things would go, but her boyfriend wasn't stupid, he stayed quiet and tried to scoot over to make room for both of them on the narrow table.

Finally, after I managed to swallow my laughter, I suggested to her that if they wanted to continue the massage, then she needed to get back on my table, or we were ending the massage early. She glared daggers at my colleague before literally stomping back over to her table. She kept her head twisted to the side, with her eyes wide open, staring at her boyfriend for the rest of the service.

After the treatment, he paid (and tipped beautifully "for our inconvenience") and left with her wrapped around his arm. I turned to my co-worker and said, "you really should use a different bottle... it sounded like you were sucking for all your worth over there.". Her face paled with realization, and I burst out laughing. "I'm pretty certain that jug was the only thing that saved you from getting punched."

She has never carried that jug around since then.

*"After nourishment, shelter, and companionship,
stories are the thing we need most in the world."*

- Sir Philip Pullman, British Author

CHAPTER 27

JUST THE TIP

The massage trade is different from any other industry out there. Especially when it comes to tipping.

Each place I have worked at does things a bit differently, but typically cash tips go into an envelope, which we have access to whenever we need it. Debit tips get paid out either weekly or biweekly. There is no rhyme or reason. I personally do not pay attention to which client tips on debit or how much.

I might know which regulars leave a $20 bill or a coffee card on the shelf in my treatment room. Some people will tip every week by secretly trying to slide a $5 bill into my hand at the receptionist desk like they are passing me drugs, other clients will tip once every three or four massages a larger amount, and others will tip a large sum once per year. Some clients like to tip with gifts or alcohol, whereas others leave cash.

Either way, tips are meant as an additional gratuity and not something that I expect or rely on. I appreciate whatever they feel I have earned... With a few exceptions.

- One gentleman left me a rather large quantity of illegal drugs as a tip, directly before a massage with a police officer.

- An elderly lady took my hands after her massage and folded them around the tip and held on to me while thanking me for the best massage that she ever had in all of her 92 years.

When she finally released me, I opened my hand to reveal a new shiny nickel. This made me smile, thinking about how much has changed in their lifetime.

- Another excuse of a man decided to leave a $50 bill on the table sitting in a pile of his baby batter. That was a tough decision about how much I desired the money. In the end, I was still building my clientele and needed the cash, so my coworkers had to listen to my profanity as I washed it and clipped it to a makeshift clothesline in the staff room.

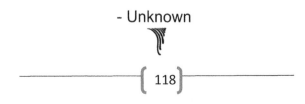

"Massage therapy – the original mood enhancer!"

- Unknown

CHAPTER 28

MEET LEONARD

When I was newer to the career, I was extra eager to try out techniques that I didn't get to use often. These were deeper tissue massage approaches that can be, well, uncomfortable (painful).

I had this male client who reminded me of Leonard from early episodes of the Big Bang Theory. He had the same characteristic thick, black-framed glasses that seemed a little too large for his sweaty plump face and an overbite, and he dressed like a college kid (despite being in his mid-late thirties). Complete with the army green backpack, low-cut black Converse All-Star sneakers, ratty jeans, and a not-quite-tan-but-not-really-brown-either jacket that has a gray hoodie integrated into it. He was rather awkward, constantly rocking on his heels during the intake, and never made small talk during his massage treatments.

The first time I met Leonard, he asked if I would spend the entire hour on just his forearms and hands! I recommend treating the surrounding muscles, maybe pecs and upper arm, but he shook his head. Ok. Just the forearms and hands.

Well, Leonard's hairy forearms were covered in thin white lines (perhaps cutting scars?) and it felt like he had a bag of frozen peas sub-dermally implanted under the skin. I had never felt so many lumps and bumps! When I asked about the pressure I was using, Leonard said he needed me to go deeper. As deep as I could.

Challenge accepted!

Typically, I gauge my client's pain tolerance by speaking with them during the treatment, but he was silent except for a couple of grunts and growls here and there as I hit an exceptionally painful area. I kept asking if the pressure was too much or if he wanted me to work lighter, but he seemed to really enjoy having me destroy the little nodules and I admit, I got lost in the anatomy of breaking down the scar tissues.

After the massage, he said I was the best, tipped me $50, and booked another massage with me for the following week. I was over the moon with pride. I had been so worried about the pressure being too painful because of all the damage in his arms. I wanted to ask him about the scars and the damage underneath but figured it was a sensitive topic and didn't want to take away from his treatment.

The next 4-5 weeks were the same. Leonard would show up for an hour on his forearms, grunt as I stripped through the knots and scar tissue (which we're feeling considerably better), tip $50, and rebook with very minimal conversation. At the end of our second to last treatment, I told him that his arms felt much looser, and he did not need weekly treatments, but he could book another massage whenever they bothered him again. He tipped me and said, "Yes, mistress!" then left. An odd comment, but I assumed he was just trying to make a joke and put the thought out of my head.

A week later, he was booked in again, and I assumed I would get to work on his back. I brought him into the treatment room and asked what brought him in so soon since his arms didn't need therapy. Without a word, he takes this weird multi-strapped whip with silver studs at the tip out of his backpack and asks me if I would flog his arms!

"Absolutely not!" I responded (a bit too loudly) and as I turned to leave the room, he fell into a submission pose and begs me not to go. I admit I should have walked away, but either curiosity or empathy got the better of me and I told him to stand up.

"Yes, mistress."

Realization hit me! He was a masochist and believed I was his Dom. I spent the next hour explaining professional boundaries, my scope of practice, and transference. I felt like I was breaking up with a potential stalker in the most delicate way possible. Thankfully, he handled it better than I expected, and left without making a scene, although I needed to take the rest of the day off to fully process what had happened.

I still can't watch Big Bang Theory without thinking that Leonard and Penny have a wild side.

"By touching a body, we touch every event it has experienced. For a few brief moments, we hold all of a client's stories in our hands... In massage therapy, we show up and ask, in so many ways, what it is like to be another human being. In doing so, we build a bridge that may heal us both."

- Tracy Walton, Massage Therapist, Researcher, Writer, and Educator

CHAPTER 29

WACKY WAVING INFLATABLE TUBE MAN

I am typically an easy-going, laid-back kind of person. I believe that laughter plays an essential part in the massage experience. I'm healing the soul as much as I am helping the body. My treatment room is a place of relaxation, humor, conversation, and sometimes harmless, good-natured flirting. The goal for everyone is to feel welcomed and comfortable.

Sometimes, however, a client will come in for a massage with "intentions" that make their massage therapist uncomfortable. Unfortunately for them, another one of my attributes is that I am really good at standing up to them. I don't become flustered or upset. And honestly, I enjoy taking them down a few pegs while reminding them that their behavior was inappropriate and unwelcome.

It was why I would get the perverts, the phallus showers, and the clients that nobody else wanted to touch. Carter was one of those clients who had been to this clinic a few times before.

The first girl he had booked a massage with was in her early twenties and a new graduate who was scared to leave the treatment early. Initially worried that she was overreacting and unsure what to do or say, she completed his treatment.

She left the massage in tears and hid in the washroom until after he had paid and left. Carter's behavior had upset her to the point that she could not finish her shift.

Because he had already left, the clinic supervisor advised her to write down everything that had happened during the treatment. The report was in his file with a yellow caution flag. Within a month, he booked an appointment online with another female therapist. She didn't notice the flag on his chart until right before he was due to arrive. As a seasoned therapist, she felt capable of diffusing any behavior he might exhibit during his session. However, when Carter began his inappropriate behavior, she promptly ended his treatment.

Although she handled herself well, she was still visibly upset. Management then decided to change the yellow caution in his file to a red flag. He would no longer be able to book his sessions online.

This didn't deter him at all. A few weeks later Carter called to book yet another session! This time, before confirming his appointment, management inquired if I would be comfortable seeing him as, at the time, I was the most experienced therapist in the clinic. I had earned a reputation for my no-nonsense personality. After reading the other therapists' notes, I eagerly agreed and began formulating my plan and counterattack.

On the day of his appointment, he arrived complaining of lower back pain and sore thighs. As I had already read his file, I knew he liked to wave his member around and touch himself during treatments. I knew that directing me to massage around that area was likely intentional on his part and I was ready for any surprises.

As I predicted, while I massaged Carter's back, he reached underneath himself and began moving his hips around. In a calm voice, I asked, "are you simply adjusting, or are you playing with your penis?" Caught off guard by my bluntness, he asked me what the difference would be. In an emotionless voice, I calmly explained that his actions would determine the outcome of the rest of his treatment. He immediately withdrew his hand and placed it at his side. I thanked him and continued his massage.

It worked for a while, but then I slowly watched as Carter once again slid his palm beneath himself. I ignored him and simply recovered his back, did some firm compressions, then instructed Carter to roll onto his back. But when he did, I saw that he was fully erect. If that wasn't enough, he then began making his penis bounce and dance like those wacky, waving inflatable tube men you see outside advertising sales.

With a smirk, he looked up at me to make sure I had noticed. I completely ignored him and his bouncing custard slinger. When it was time to work on his inner legs, I picked up the hand that he had put under himself earlier (making sure to hold the wrist in case his hand was damp) and placed it directly on top of his dancing penis (pushing down just a little bit aggressively). I ordered him to keep his hand there, as I had had enough of his nonsense.

Carter tried to play stupid by asking what I was talking about; I looked down at him and warned him that if he moved his hand, I would leave the room, and I would be taking his clothing with me. I warned him that I had done this with a previous client who had gotten handsy and I had no problem doing it again. He laughed, then stopped when he realized I was serious.

From that moment on, the rest of his massage was mostly uneventful. He tried making a few comments intended to make me uncomfortable, asking about happy endings, but I cheerfully answered that everyone leaves in a great mood. He eventually realized he wasn't getting the rise from me he was looking for, and the rest of his session was in blissful quiet.

When he came out to pay, he was topless. Another attempt. Everybody was astonished that not only did I not react, but I recommended he put his shirt on "because it's chilly outside." I also encouraged him to book another appointment, which made him stop and stare at me before stuttering that no one had ever offered a second appointment. I laughed and said, "I can't imagine why?" I walked back to my treatment room, praying there were no surprises on the sheets.

During my follow-up with management, I recommended that the warning stays in his file and that they do not book him with any female therapists except myself in the future. I added my experience to his chart along with the recommendation.

Months later, Carter showed up without an appointment and apologized profusely for his previous actions. He also shared that he had been banned at every spa and clinic in the city for his antics. And that I was the only massage therapist that had called him out on his behavior. Carter then admitted he had pulled his groin muscle at work and could not find anywhere else that would treat him.

Karma is so wonderful!

I agreed to treat him as long as he behaved himself as promised. Indeed, he had pulled the tendon and was in significant pain. Since then, he has become the perfect client because he knows he has no other option.

" Compassion is a bridge between the client and the therapist. It can be argued that without compassion, no healing takes place. Not only is compassion a bridge, but it is also the container for the therapeutic relationship."

- Susan Salvo, Massage Therapy Principles and Practice

CHAPTER 30

HAPPY ENDINGS

W hen people jokingly ask if I give happy endings I cheerfully reply, "Of course I do! All my clients have happy endings. They come in feeling pain and leave either pain-free or in less pain. They arrived to me feeling stressed out and leave less stressed and much happier. Massage therapy has many benefits, happiness is one of them, thanks for asking."

"I am a pain-removing health improving back repairing always caring muscle kneading stress relieving miracle working massage therapist."

- Unknown

"A Different Kind of Happy Ending"

Illustrated by Kierra Boutilier
© 2022

Referenced from @ChrisHallbeck original comic

CHAPTER 31

THE END?

What a wonderful career massage therapy is!

Over the past twenty years, I have seen the profession develop, grow, and evolve. We are slowly gaining recognition as Real Healthcare Professionals. We are no longer treated like the unwanted little brother who tags along behind all the older cool kids.

Treatment environments have expanded from nail salons and spas to clinical settings and multidisciplinary teams, with more and more options for professional development every few years.

I have spent a lot of time thinking about what massage therapy has in common with other paramedical healthcare professions. Our skills and education all focus around and sometimes overlap with, Physiotherapists, Occupational Therapists, Osteopaths, Kinesiologists, and Chiropractors. And I am certain that there are more.

So, what makes us different from them? What sets us apart? What makes us unique?

Touch!

It is our training and experience in palpation in ways rarely used by others. It is the variety and quality of touch – the speed, breadth, depth, and intention. The magnitude of various types of massage, from Swedish to Deep Tissue, relaxation to unwind, or vigorous to pump up before a sporting event. It's how we can connect body to body, person to person, using our fingers, hands, forearms, feet, elbows, whatever is needed, and is most effective in many varied situations to create a treatment that is as unique as the person we are helping.

It is the unspoken dialogue that happens between the client and the therapist through the various muscles and tissues. Furthermore, it is also the heart and soul that can only be expressed and communicated through touch that truly sets us apart from other professionals and makes us such a valuable part of the multitude of similar professions.

This is why I love massage therapy. I wrote this book to show you the good, the bad, the perverted, and the messy. Completely Raw and 100% Real. I hope you have enjoyed reading this book as much as I have enjoyed writing it.

I can't wait to get started on Book 2.

"Confessions of a Massage Clinic – True stories from Other Massage Therapists."

Until then, I leave you with these words:

"By touching a body, we touch every event it has experienced. For a few brief moments, we hold all of a client's stories in our hands...In massage therapy, we show up and ask, in so many ways, what it is like to be another human being. In doing so, we build a bridge that may heal us both."

- Tracy Walton, Pioneer in oncology massage and author of "The Healing History of the Human Being" and many more titles.

Changing lives...
ONE APPOINTMENT AT A TIME

How To Contact The Author

For additional massage-related humour, and updates on the progress of Book2- follow my Instagram page:

https://instagram.com/krista_wright_rmt?r=nametag

Www.Instagram.com/Krista_Wright_RMT

If you are a massage therapist and have a similar experience you would like to share, please email me at:

Krista-Wright82@live.com

REFERENCES

Bateman, Jason. (August 19, 2022) www.quotefancy.com

Breault, Robert. (August 2022) www.quotefancy.com

Brown, Angela Laverne. (August 15, 2022) www. brainyquote.com

Calvert, Robert Noah. (August 4, 2022) www.massageschoolnotes.com

Desmond, Viola. (August 17, 2022) www.searchquotes.com

Fakhri, Nargis. (August 2022) www.brainyquote.com

Field, Tiffany. (August 2022) www.massagemag.com

Juhan, Deane. Job's Body: A Handbook for Bodywork. (August 14, 2022) www.massageschoolnotes.com/

Matteo, Jesse and Bryan Matteo. (August 4, 2022) www.thecorelinksolution.com

Meagher, Jack (August 14, 2022) www.azquotes.com

Morrison, Toni. www.Richlandlibrary.com blog- *A tribute to Toni Morrison*

Pullman, Philip. (2008) *The Book of Rumy*

Roberts, Nora. (August 2022) Dark Witch (The Cousins O'Dwyer Trilogy, #1))www.goodreads.com

Salvo, Susan. (1999) *Massage Therapy Principles and Practice.* https://www.massageschoolnotes.com

Smith, Irene. (August 17, 2022) www.solvidamassage.com

Spanish Proverb. (August 4, 2022) www.discoverquotes.com

The Random Vibez (August 4, 2022) www.therandomvibez.com

Unknown. (August 2022) www.ambientnoise.online

Unknown. (August 4, 2022) www.amazon.com/FACT-CRACKS-STICK-WHENEVER-T-Shirt

Vardaxis, Dr. Nicholas. (August 4, 2022) www.wisesayings.com

Walton, Tracy. (August 19, 2022) https://www.tracywalton.com

Words of Wisdom (Oct 2010) www.blogs.smith.edu.

Wendig, Chuck. (August 4, 2022) www.twitter.com/chuckwendig

Made in the USA
Columbia, SC
16 October 2022

69508770R00085